EMOTIONAL INTELLIGENT

WHAT IT TAKES TO BE AND WHY IT IS IMPORTANT

KAMAL HUSSAIN

Made with ♥ on the Notion Press Platform
www.notionpress.com

Parents and Teacher who taught me the basic of life Science and to the millions of researchers who are making the best practices of knowledge to serve the Humankind.

- Kamal Hussain

Contents

Foreword

Emotional intelligence is a key competency for successful working relationships, personal happiness and business success. In today's fast-paced work environment, your emotional intelligence can make all the difference to your career and happiness.

This book shows you how to identify, manage and develop your emotional intelligence skills. The author has guide different definition and approach to understand and deals with human emotional intelligence.

The author of the book has written a book title "Human mind and machine" which deals with human and machine cognitive; and this book title Emotional Intelligence (What it takes to be and why it is important) shows his another deep knowledge.

He holds professional certifications in the field of Computers Science, Digital Thinking Tools for Better Decision Making - from United Kingdom. He has actively participated in the enduring material title "Mental Health Effect of Covid-19 pandemic" from Harvard Medical School, Boston, United States, to understand human cogitative state during pandemic and Health emergency program from World Health Organization to analysis and understand the emerging respiratory viruses, including covid-19, method for detection, prevention, response and control to analyze human state of mind.This book provides an outline of human mind and emotional intelligence, and will be of interest to a wide range of readers.

25th Jan, 2023, Dr. Shazen | (Psychology),France

Preface

Human mind and its intelligence has always been a subject of research. Human has developed it interpersonal skills and has adopted a change from primitive to modern age. These adaptabilities of social skill sets and social intelligence have played a significant role. In the age of modern era where sharp societal changes are taking place, understanding human intelligence and its emotion play a vital role. This Book gives us knowledge about human emotional intelligence. I kept it open for a reader to understand the ideology of emotional intelligence from basic to core for self development and for others.

The concept of emotional intelligence has been applied to many different fields of work, including healthcare, finance and education. By understanding how emotions influence the behavior within an organization, one can better manage emotions and those of others for progressive outcome. It gives us a philosophical approach to understand and develop emotional intelligence by helping to manage emotion in a healthy way.

This book is intended for professional psychologists, counselors, manager, leader, educators, students and any individual who wish to understand the importance of emotional intelligence and its connection to competence in their professional roles. A comprehensive overview of theory and research, it provides information on measurement issues, common problems in assessment and guidance for those looking to build their assessment tools.

Kamal Hussain

Acknowledgements

Writing this book on emotional intelligence has been a love for me, and I appreciate all the help and guidance I have received along the way.I am truly grateful for the support I have received from my peers and peers in the field of emotional intelligence. There analysis and insights have been an invaluable resource in the outcome of this book.

I thank my family and friends for their unwavering support and encouragement."I would also like to express my gratitude to the researchers and scientists who are referenced cited in this book. Their contributions in the field of Emotional intelligence have greatly contributed to shaping the topic.

I would also like to thank the librarians and staff of the research institutes and libraries where I carry out my research for their help and support. I would like to acknowledge the support of my organization and the agency that supported this work. Their support helped me conduct the research and write this book.

I would like to acknowledge the family of Lt. Dr. Charles P. Alexander whose Book title "Clinical Philosophy" is the key component for writing this book.

Finally, I would like to thank the readers of this book for their interest in the topic of emotional intelligence. We hope this book will provide valuable information and encourage further exploration and research in the field of emotional intelligence.

CHAPTER I

Understanding Emotions

Emotions are mental states produced by neuro physiological changes that are associated in various ways with thoughts, feelings, behavioral responses, and to some extent pleasure or displeasure. It is natural and important part of the human experiences.

It is also defined as feelings that are accompanied by physiological and personal significance of a thing, an event, or a state of affairs or behavioral changes. They are typically short-lived and are triggered by specific events or situations. There are many different types of emotions, including happiness, sadness, anger, fear, and love.

Each emotion serves a specific purpose, such as helping us to avoid danger or form of social connections. They are complex and multi-dimensional which influence our thoughts and behaviors. Understanding emotions is crucial for managing them effectively and leading a fulfilling life.

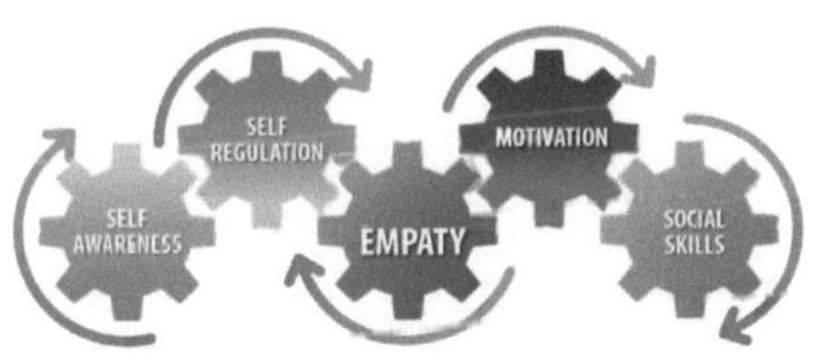

Fig 1.1 (Intelligence -Stages)

Emotion process

Emotions are processed in the brain through a complex network of structures. The limbic system, which includes the amygdala and the hypothalamus, plays a key role in the processing of emotions. The amygdala is responsible for the rapid detection of emotionally significant stimuli and the initiation of the body's emotional response. The hypothalamus is responsible for the regulation of physiological responses to emotions, such as heart rate and blood pressure.

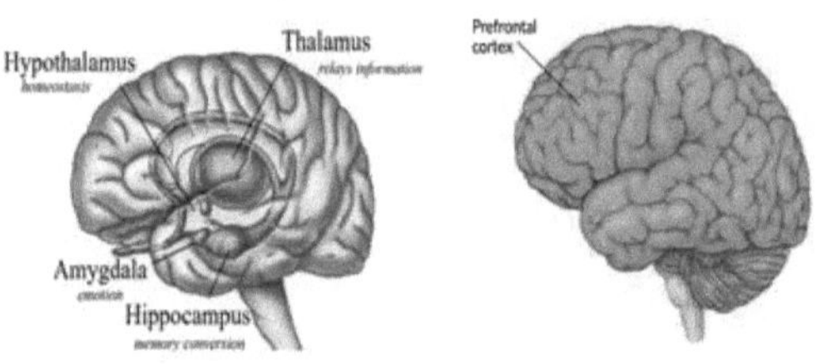

Fig 1.2 (The Limbic System)

Emotions also have a cognitive component, which is processed in the prefrontal cortex. This is the part of the brain responsible for higher-level thinking and decision making. The prefrontal cortex plays a role in the regulation of emotions and the ability to think about them in a more reflective and detached manner. They also play a role in personality expression and creativity.

These skills are known collectively as **executive functions**. Executive functions are higher cognitive processes that help us control our impulses and act with long-term consequences in mind. They allow us to interact with others in appropriate ways and adjust our behavior to fit the circumstances.Some more specific examples of executive functions include anticipation, initiation, self-monitoring, and self-correction. Unfortunately, a frontal lobe injury can cause a decrease in most of these functions.

Classification of Emotions

Classifications of Emotion are broader area of research and discussion in scientific community till today, yet some research line by research community has drawn which helps research community to understand human emotions.

Emotions can be positive or negative. Positive emotions, such as happiness and love, are associated with feelings of pleasure and well-being. Negative emotions, such as anger and fear, are associated with feelings of discomfort and distress. Both positive and negative emotions are important and serve different functions. Positive emotions help us to form social connections and cope with stress, while negative emotions help us to avoid danger and cope with difficult situations.

Emotions can also be primary or secondary. Primary emotions are those that are experienced immediately in response to a specific event or situation, such as feeling happy when receiving a compliment. Secondary emotions are those that are experienced after reflecting on a primary emotion, such as feeling proud after feeling happy about receiving a compliment.

Emotions can also be categorized into basic or complex. Basic emotions are those that are innate and universal, such as happiness, sadness, and fear. Complex emotions are those that are learned and specific to a culture or individual, such as guilt or shame.

Emotions can also be displayed in different ways. **There are two main ways in which emotions are displayed: verbally and non-verbally.** Verbal displays of emotions include words and tone of voice, while nonverbal displays of emotions include facial expressions, body language, and physiological responses. Often these emotions play vital role in one day to day activity in human life

Fig 1.3 (verbally and non-verbally-emotion)

Significant role of Emotions

Emotions also play a significant role in our relationships and interactions with others. They can impact how we communicate and connect with others, and they can influence how we respond to others' emotions. Emotional intelligence, which is the ability to recognize and understand one's own emotions and the emotions of others, is an important factor in successful relationships and interactions.

Furthermore, emotions can also have a significant impact on our physical health. Chronic stress and negative emotions such as anger and anxiety can lead to a variety of health problems, including heart disease, high blood pressure, and depression. On the other hand, positive emotions such as happiness and love can have a positive impact on our physical health, boosting the immune system and reducing the risk of illness.

Emotions can also be influenced by external factors such as culture, upbringing, and life experiences. Cultural norms and expectations can shape how emotions are expressed and perceived, and individual life experiences can also shape how one processes and responds to emotions. For example, a person who has experienced trauma may have a heightened emotional response to certain triggers as a result of their past experiences.It's also important to note that emotions are not always rational or logical. They can be triggered by a wide range of factors, both internal and external, and may not always align with our thoughts or beliefs. It's important to recognize this and not to blame oneself for feeling a certain way.It's also worth noting that everyone has different ways of coping with emotions and what works for one person may not work for another. It's important to find what works for you and to be open to trying new things.

Additionally, it's important to recognize that it's normal to have ups and downs, and that emotions are not always constant. They come and go, and that is normal.One way to manage emotions is through mindfulness techniques. Mindfulness is the practice of being present in the moment and focusing on one's thoughts and feelings without judgment. Mindfulness can help to increase awareness of emotions and can also help to reduce negative emotions such as anxiety and depression. Mindfulness can be practiced through meditation, yoga, or other forms of relaxation.

Another way to manage emotions is through cognitive-behavioral therapy (CBT). CBT is a form of therapy that focuses on identifying and changing negative thought patterns and beliefs that can contribute to emotional distress. It can be helpful for individuals who struggle with negative emotions such as anxiety and depression.Additionally, it's important to take care of oneself physically, emotionally and mentally. This includes getting enough sleep, eating well, and engaging in regular physical activity. It also includes finding healthy outlets for emotions such as journaling, talking to friends, or participating in a hobby. And also, it's important to have a support system of people you can talk to, who can help you when you're struggling.

In summary, emotions are a complex and multi-dimensional aspect of human experience that have a significant impact on our thoughts, behaviors, relationships, and physical health. Understanding emotions and finding ways to manage them effectively is crucial for leading a fulfilling life. This includes recognizing and labeling emotions, developing emotional intelligence, practicing mindfulness, seeking therapy if needed, taking care of oneself and having a support system. And it's important to remember that everyone is different, and what works for one person may not work for another, so it's important to find what works for you.

CHAPTER II

The Origins of Emotional Intelligence

Factors classified as "**emotional intelligence**" were first discussed under "**Social Intelligence**". The term was later combined with 'emotional intelligence' to form the generic term 'emotional and social intelligence'.

The Emotional Intelligence term was first coined by Wayne Payne (1986). He invented the term Emotional intelligence in his doctoral dissertation "*Study of Emotion: Development of Emotional Intelligence*", self-integration,¨ Associated with fear, pain and desire.

In his work, Payne studied the nature and characteristics of emotion and emotional intelligence. He discovered that the world was suffering from ¨emotional ignorance¨ , where many of the problems society was facing were related to emotional states like depression, addiction, fear, pain, etc. He realized that courses where the nature of emotions and emotions themselves were taught did not really exist; his work laid the groundwork for the emergence of the next researcher this field.

Wayne Payne's assertions opened up a new field where a great discovery was made. In his thesis,Payne sought to create a guide to help individuals to develop emotional intelligence and outline.Continuing with **Wayne Payne's work, Peter Sarovay** and **John D. Mayer** used the term "emotional intelligence" again.In 1990, he stated that EI is "a form of social intelligence that includes the ability to monitor oneself and others."

This definition was later classified into four proposed abilities: perceiving, using, understanding, and managing emotions. These abilities are manifest yet related. However, certain disagreement exists regarding the definition of EI, with respect to both terminology and operationalization's.

Presently, there are three main models of EI:

- Ability model
- Mixed model (usually subsumed under trait EI)
- Trait model

But it wasn't until 1990 that Daniel Goleman published his book Emotional Intelligence, why **EI** matter more.As **IQ**¨, the concept of **EI** has become a part of socio-culture and has begun to be applied worldwide (Goleman, 1998).

Today, the term play an important role in understanding human behaviors that it proudly sits at the point between management and psychology, making it one of the most important skills in any professional's portfolio. But how was this term conceived and devised? How did it end up in research journals and popular literature? Let's find out.

History of Emotional Intelligence

- **1930s** - Edward Thorndyke described the concept of social intelligence as the ability to get along with other people by understanding one's own and others' internal states, motivations and behaviors.
- **1940s** - David Wechsler developed the concept of non-cognitive intelligence and said intelligence was essential to success in life until he was able to define the non-cognitive dimension.
- **1950s** - Humanistic psychologist Abraham Maslow suggested humans could build emotional strength
- **1975** – Howard Gardner introduced the concept of multiple intelligences in his book The Shattered Mind.
- **1983** – Howard Gardner introduced interpersonal and intrapersonal intelligence in his book Frames of Mind and said it was as important as IQ
- **1985** - Wayne Payne, "The Study of Emotions: Development of Emotional Intelligence; Self-Integration; (Theory, Structure of Reality, Problem Solving, Contraction/Expansion, Entrainment/Consequences/Release)"- Ph.D. Thesis

- **1987** - Mensa magazine, Keith Beasley uses the term "emotional quotient". In an article published in **unpublished version of his paper.**
- **1990** - Psychologists Peter Salovey and John Mayer publish a seminal paper, "Emotional Intelligence," in the journal Imagination, Cognition, and Personality.
- **1995** - The concept of EI became popular after the publication of Daniel Goleman's book Emotional Intelligence: Why It Can Matter More than IQ.

Development in Emotions and Intelligence in Past Century
1900-1969: Intelligence and Emotions as Separate Narrow Fields
1. Intelligence Research

- Psychometric approaches to intelligence are developed and refined.

2. Emotions Research

- Debate which comes first: physiological or emotional response.
- The movement of Darwin's theory on the heritability and evolution of emotional responses has so far been considered culturally determined.
- Social intelligence as an introduced concept.

1970-1989 - Precursors to EI

- The field of Cognition and Emotion has emerged to study how emotions interact with thoughts.
- Gardner's theory of multiple intelligences explained intrapersonal intelligence and interpersonal intelligence.
- Empirical research on social intelligence has developed her four components: social skills, empathic skills, platitudes, and emotions (sensitivity).

- Brain research is beginning to reveal the relationship between emotion and cognition.
- Occasional use of EI appeared.

1990-1993 - The Emergence of EI

- Mayer and Salovey have published a series of articles on EI.
- EI's first proficiency measurements have been released.
- The editor of Intelligence magazine claimed the existence of EI.
- His EI advances in brain science.

1994-1997 - The Popularization and Broadening

- Goleman publishes Emotional Intelligence, a worldwide bestseller.
- Time magazine used the term 'EQ' on its cover
- EI measurement using mixed model theory is published.

1998 - Research on the Institutionalization of EI

- Improved EI concept.
- Introduced new measures for EI.
- Appearance of peer-reviewed articles on this topic.

Concept and Theory

There are many authors who have made significant contributions to EI research. This chapter examines only three models in brief. All of them help to make sense of EI.

1. **Salovey-Mayer model** - This model proposes that four fundamental emotion-related abilities comprise EI: (1) perception/expression of emotion, (2) use of emotion to facilitate thinking, (3) understanding of emotion, and (4) management of emotion in oneself and others.

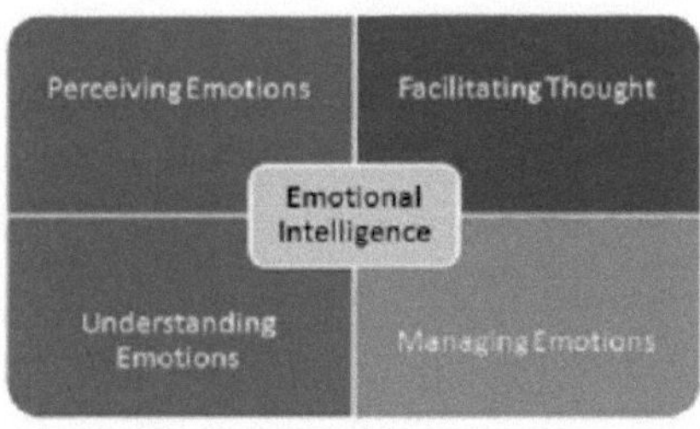

Fig1.1 (Salovey-Mayer model)

2. **Goleman's model** -This model outlines five components of EQ: self-awareness, self-regulation, motivation, empathy, and social skills.

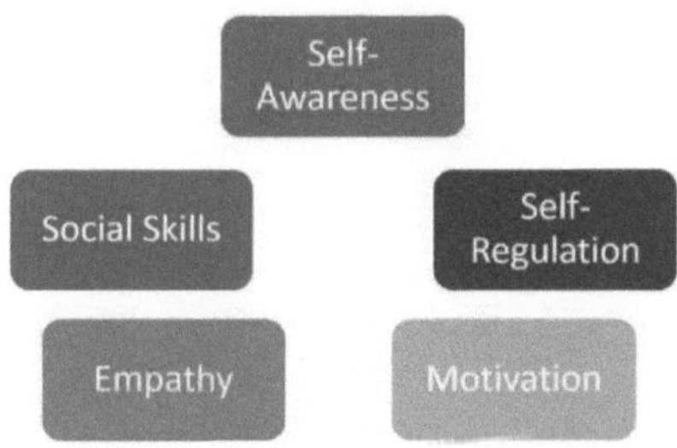

Fig1.2 (Goleman's model)

3. A **Bar-On Model** This model has five main markers namely:Interpersonal,Decision-making,Self-expression,Self-participation,Stress management

   These are further divided into 15 representative subdivisions:

- Interpersonal relationships, empathy, social responsibility
- Problem-solving, reality testing, impulse control
- Emotional expression, assertiveness, independence
- Self-regard, self-actualization, emothional self awereness
- Flexibility, stress tolerence,and optimism Moderators who influence intellectual behavior as measured by self-assessment.

Nowadays, it can be assumed that emotional intelligence has gained relevance in almost every corner of the world. It has raised the interest of many people and researchers who have written many magazines, books, newspaper articles, scientific experiments, etc.. Furthermore, if the words emotional intelligence are entered into Google the searcher finds as many as 10, 50, 00,000 (27 Jan 2023) results, which shows how EI forms a fundamental part of today´s society.

CHAPTER III

Recognizing Emotions in Yourself

Being able to recognize and understand your own emotions is a crucial step in managing them effectively. It allows you to identify what you are feeling, understand the cause of those feelings, and take appropriate action. This chapter will focus on ways to become more aware of your own emotions and how they manifest in your thoughts, behaviors, and physical sensations.

One way to increase awareness of your emotions is through mindfulness practices. Mindfulness is the practice of being present in the moment and paying attention to one's thoughts and feelings without judgment. By practicing mindfulness, you can become more aware of your emotions as they arise and learn to observe them without getting caught up in them. Mindfulness can be practiced through meditation, yoga, or other forms of relaxation.

Another way to increase awareness of your emotions is by keeping a journal. Writing down your thoughts and feelings can help you to identify patterns and triggers for certain emotions. It can also serve as a helpful tool for reflecting on your emotions and understanding how they have affected you over time.

It's also important to learn how to identify and label your emotions. This can be challenging, as emotions can be complex and multi-faceted. However, being able to identify and label your emotions can help you to understand them better and take appropriate action. The following are some common emotions and their corresponding physical sensations and behaviors:

- Anger: tightness in the chest, clenched jaw, feelings of frustration or irritability
- Anxiety: racing heart, muscle tension, feelings of worry or nervousness
- Happiness: feeling light and carefree, smiling, positive energy

- Sadness: feeling heavy and low, tearfulness, feeling hopeless

Additionally, understanding the cause of your emotions can be helpful in managing them. For example, if you are feeling anxious, try to identify the source of that anxiety. Is it a specific event or situation that is causing the anxiety? Or is it something more general such as a belief or thought pattern? By understanding the cause of your emotions, you can take steps to address the root of the problem and manage the emotions more effectively.

It's also important to recognize that emotions are not always rational or logical. They can be triggered by a wide range of factors, both internal and external, and may not always align with our thoughts or beliefs. It's important to recognize this and not to blame oneself for feeling a certain way.

Furthermore, it's important to recognize that emotions are not constant, they come and go. And it's normal to experience a wide range of emotions. It's not always possible or healthy to suppress or eliminate negative emotions. It's important to allow yourself to feel the emotions and to process them in a healthy way.

Recognizing Emotions in Yourself

What is the relationship between thoughts, emotions and behaviors'?

Thoughts and emotions are closely related, as thoughts can often lead to strong emotional reactions. How we think about things can directly affect how we feel, and vice versa.For example, if you are under a lot of stress at work, you will feel anxious and nervous all the time. This fear can lead to negative thoughts. Believing that you are not good enough or will never be able to handle the stress.These thoughts only fuel the emotional state and make it even harder to get out of. Conversely, if you have a positive attitude and believe you can handle anything, you are more likely to feel less stressed and more confident in your abilities. This trust leads to happier thoughts and feelings.In short, our thoughts have a powerful influence on our emotions, which determine our actions.

Fig 1.1 (Recognizing emotions in yourself)

Another important aspect of recognizing emotions in yourself is being able to distinguish between emotions and thoughts. Emotions are feelings that are accompanied by physiological and behavioral changes, while thoughts are mental events, such as ideas, beliefs, or judgments. It's important to recognize that thoughts can influence emotions, but they are not the same thing. Being able to distinguish between emotions and thoughts can help you to understand the cause of your emotions better, and can also be helpful in reframing negative thoughts.

Another important aspect of recognizing emotions in yourself is being able to recognize the intensity and duration of emotions. Emotions can range from mild to intense, and can last for a short or long period of time. Recognizing the intensity and duration of emotions can help you to understand the impact of the emotions on your thoughts, behaviors, and physical sensations. It can also help you to determine the most appropriate response to the emotions.

Additionally, recognizing emotions in yourself includes understanding the role of physiological responses in emotions. Emotions are accompanied by physiological changes such as increased heart rate, sweating, and muscle tension. Recognizing these physiological responses can help you to identify the emotions that you are experiencing and to understand the cause of those emotions. It can also be helpful in managing the emotions, as certain physiological responses can be reduced through relaxation techniques such as deep breathing and progressive muscle relaxation.

It's also important to recognize the role of past experiences in emotions. Our past experiences can shape how we process and respond to emotions. For example, if someone has experienced trauma in the past, they may have a heightened emotional response to certain triggers as a result of their past experiences. Recognizing the role of past experiences in emotions can help you to understand why you may be experiencing certain emotions and can also be helpful in managing those emotions.

Another important aspect of recognizing emotions in yourself is being able to differentiate between emotions and needs. Emotions are feelings that arise in response to certain events or situations, while needs are more fundamental and enduring. Emotions can be a signal that a need is not being met. For example, feeling angry might signal a need for respect or fairness. By identifying the underlying need that is not being met, you can take steps to address it and manage the emotion more effectively.

Another important aspect of recognizing emotions in yourself is being able to recognize the role of emotions in decision making. Emotions can influence decision making in both positive and negative ways. Positive emotions such as happiness and excitement can lead to more positive and optimistic decision making, while negative emotions such as anger and fear can lead to more negative and impulsive decision making. Recognizing the role of emotions in decision making can help you to make more rational and objective decisions, despite the influence of emotions.

Additionally, recognizing emotions in yourself includes understanding the role of social context in emotions. Social context refers to the influence of other people and the environment on emotions. For example, the emotions of others can influence our own emotions through a process known as emotional contagion, where emotions spread from one person to another. Additionally, the environment can also influence emotions, such as feeling more relaxed in a peaceful and quiet environment compared to a loud and chaotic one. Recognizing the role of social context in emotions can help you to understand why you may be experiencing certain emotions and can also be helpful in managing those emotions.

It's also important to recognize that emotions can change over time. Emotions are not static and can change in response to different events or situations. Recognizing that emotions can change over time can help you to understand that emotions are not permanent and that it's possible to feel differently in the future.

Recognizing emotions in yourself is a crucial step in managing them effectively. It includes becoming more aware of your emotions through mindfulness practices, keeping a journal, identifying and labeling emotions, understanding the cause of emotions, recognizing that emotions are not always rational or logical, and allowing yourself to feel a wide range of emotions without judging yourself. It also includes understanding the role of thoughts, intensity and duration of emotions, physiological responses, and past experiences in emotions. If you find that you are struggling to manage your emotions, seeking help from a therapist or counselor can be beneficial. It's important to remember that mastering emotions is a lifelong journey and that it's normal to have ups and downs, but with the right tools and mindset, you can learn to manage them in a healthy way.

CHAPTER IV

Managing Emotions

Managing emotions is an essential aspect of leading a fulfilling and healthy life. It involves being able to recognize and understand one's own emotions, as well as taking appropriate action to address them. This chapter will focus on strategies for managing emotions effectively.

One of the most effective ways to manage emotions is through mindfulness practices. Mindfulness is the practice of being present in the moment and paying attention to one's thoughts and feelings without judgment. By practicing mindfulness, you can become more aware of your emotions as they arise and learn to observe them without getting caught up in them. This can help to reduce negative emotions such as anxiety and depression, and increase positive emotions such as happiness and love. Mindfulness can be practiced through meditation, yoga, or other forms of relaxation.

Cognitive-Behavioral Therapy (CBT)

Emotions can be managed through cognitive-behavioral therapy (CBT). CBT is a form of therapy that focuses on identifying and changing negative thought patterns and beliefs that can contribute to emotional distress. By identifying and changing these negative thoughts, individuals can learn to manage negative emotions such as anxiety and depression more effectively.

Additionally, managing emotions involves learning how to cope with difficult emotions in a healthy way. This includes learning how to express emotions in a healthy way, such as through journaling, talking to friends, or participating in a hobby. It also includes learning how to regulate emotions, such as through deep breathing exercises, progressive muscle relaxation, and other relaxation techniques.

Self-Compassion

Important aspect of managing emotions is self-compassion. Self-compassion involves treating oneself with kindness and understanding when experiencing difficult emotions. It involves recognizing that it's normal to experience a wide range of emotions, and that everyone has ups and downs. It also involves recognizing that emotions are not always rational or logical, and that it's not always possible or healthy to suppress or eliminate negative emotions.

Furthermore, managing emotions also involves setting boundaries and learning how to say no. This can be difficult, especially if you're a people pleaser or if you find it hard to say no to others. However, setting boundaries is important in order to protect your emotional well-being. You deserve to be treated with respect and kindness, and it's important to set boundaries with others when necessary.

Another important aspect of managing emotions is learning how to forgive. Forgiveness is the process of letting go of feelings of resentment or anger towards someone who has hurt you. Forgiveness can be difficult, but it's an important aspect of emotional well-being. By forgiving others, you can let go of negative emotions that may be holding you back and move forward in a more positive direction.

Setting and Achieving Goals

Emotions can also be managed by learning how to set and achieve goals. Setting and achieving goals can help to increase feelings of self-efficacy and self-worth, which can in turn help to reduce negative emotions such as anxiety and depression. Setting and achieving goals can also provide a sense of purpose and direction, which can be helpful in managing difficult emotions. Managing emotions can be achieved learning how to prioritize self-care.

Self-care includes taking care of oneself physically, emotionally and mentally. This includes getting enough sleep, eating well, and engaging in regular physical activity. It also includes finding healthy outlets for emotions such as journaling, talking to friends, or participating in a hobby. Additionally, it's important to have a support system of people you can talk to, who can help you when you're struggling.

Emotion regulation

Managing emotions also involves learning how to regulate emotions through emotions regulation techniques. Emotion regulation is the process of changing one's emotional response to a situation. There are several techniques that can be used to regulate emotions, such as cognitive reappraisal, which involves changing the way you think about a situation in order to change the way you feel about it.

Another technique is expressive writing, which involves writing about your emotions in order to better understand and process them.Furthermore, managing emotions also involves learning how to communicate effectively. Effective communication involves being able to express oneself clearly and respectfully, while also being able to listen actively and empathically to others. Effective communication can help to reduce conflicts and misunderstandings, and can help to increase feelings of connectedness and understanding.

Another important aspect of managing emotions is learning how to deal with difficult people and situations. We all encounter people and situations that are challenging and that can trigger negative emotions. It's important to learn how to deal with these people and situations in a healthy way, without getting caught up in negative emotions. This can include setting boundaries, learning how to communicate effectively, and practicing mindfulness and self-compassion.Managing emotions also involves learning how to identify and challenge negative thoughts and beliefs. Negative thoughts and beliefs can contribute to negative emotions, such as anxiety and depression. Identifying and challenging negative thoughts and beliefs can help to reduce negative emotions and increase positive emotions.

Taking perspective

Additionally, managing emotions involves learning how to take perspective. Taking perspective means looking at a situation from different angles, and considering different perspectives. It can help to reduce negative emotions, such as anger and frustration, and increase positive emotions, such as understanding and empathy.

Another important aspect of managing emotions is learning how to manage stress. Stress can contribute to negative emotions and can have a negative impact on physical and mental health. It's important to learn how to manage stress in a healthy way, through techniques such as deep breathing, progressive muscle relaxation, and mindfulness.

Managing emotions is an essential aspect of leading a fulfilling and healthy life. It involves being able to recognize and understand one's own emotions, as well as taking appropriate action to address them. This can include practicing mindfulness, seeking therapy, learning to cope with difficult emotions in a healthy way, self-compassion, setting boundaries, learning how to forgive, setting and achieving goals, prioritizing self-care, regulating emotions, learning how to communicate effectively, dealing with difficult people and situations, identifying and challenging negative thoughts and beliefs, taking perspective, and managing stress.

Remember that mastering emotions is a lifelong journey and that it's normal to have ups and downs. However, with the right tools and mindset, you can learn to manage them in a healthy way. Additionally, it's important to keep in mind that everyone is different, and what works for one person may not work for another, so it's important to find what works for you

CHAPTER V

Building Emotional Intelligence

Building emotional intelligence is an important aspect of managing emotions, as it can help to improve relationships, increase self-awareness, and reduce stress and negative emotions. This chapter will focus on strategies for building emotional intelligence.

Mindfulness practice

One of the most effective ways to build emotional intelligence is through mindfulness practices. Mindfulness is the practice of being present in the moment and paying attention to one's thoughts and feelings without judgment. By practicing mindfulness, individuals can become more aware of their own emotions, as well as the emotions of others. This can help to improve empathy and communication, and can also help to increase self-awareness. Mindfulness can be practiced through meditation, yoga, or other forms of relaxation.

Another way to build emotional intelligence is through active listening. Active listening is the process of paying attention and responding to what others are saying, both verbally and non-verbally. By actively listening to others, individuals can improve their ability to empathize and understand the emotions of others. This can help to improve communication and relationships.Additionally, building emotional intelligence involves learning how to regulate emotions, both in oneself and in others. This includes learning how to express emotions in a healthy way, as well as learning how to manage the emotions of others. It also includes learning how to de-escalate conflicts and how to respond in a calm and effective way to difficult situations.

Self-compassion

Another important aspect of building emotional intelligence is self-compassion. Self-compassion involves treating oneself with kindness and understanding when experiencing difficult emotions.

It involves recognizing that it's normal to experience a wide range of emotions, and that everyone has ups and downs. It also involves recognizing that emotions are not always rational or logical, and that it's not always possible or healthy to suppress or eliminate negative emotions.

Furthermore, building emotional intelligence also involves setting boundaries and learning how to say no and setting these boundaries is important in order to protect your emotional well-being. You deserve to be treated with respect and kindness, and it's important to set boundaries with others when necessary.

Manage Stress

Additionally, building emotional intelligence also involves learning how to manage stress. Stress can have a negative impact on emotional intelligence, as it can make it more difficult to recognize and manage emotions. It's important to learn how to manage stress in a healthy way, through techniques such as deep breathing, progressive muscle relaxation, and mindfulness.

Another important aspect of building emotional intelligence is learning how to recognize and manage emotions in others. This includes being able to identify the emotions of others, as well as understanding the causes and triggers of those emotions. It also includes learning how to respond to the emotions of others in a supportive and appropriate way.Furthermore, building emotional intelligence also involves learning how to take responsibility for one's emotions. This means recognizing that we are responsible for our own emotions, and that we have the power to change them. It also means recognizing that we are not responsible for the emotions of others.

Maintain Healthy Relationships

Another important aspect of building emotional intelligence is learning how to build and maintain healthy relationships. This includes learning how to communicate effectively, empathize, and build trust with others. Building and maintaining healthy relationships can help to increase emotional intelligence as it allows for better understanding and management of emotions in oneself and others.

Additionally, building emotional intelligence involves learning how to manage emotions in different social and cultural contexts. Emotions can be expressed differently across cultures and it's important to learn and understand these differences in order to navigate social interactions effectively.It's also important to recognize that building emotional intelligence is a continuous process and it requires continuous effort to maintain it. It's important to regularly evaluate and reflect on one's emotional intelligence, and continuously work on improving it.

Criticism and Feedback

Another important aspect of building emotional intelligence is learning how to handle criticism and feedback. Criticism and feedback can be difficult to handle and can trigger negative emotions such as anger, frustration or sadness. However, learning how to handle criticism and feedback in a constructive way can help to improve emotional intelligence as it allows for better understanding and management of emotions, and also helps to improve self-awareness.

It's also important to learn how to manage and express emotions in a professional setting. Emotions can be challenging to handle in a professional setting, but learning how to express emotions in a professional manner can help to improve emotional intelligence, as it allows for better understanding and management of emotions, and also helps to improve communication and relationships in a professional setting.

Conflicts

Another important aspect of building emotional intelligence is learning how to manage emotions in conflict situations. Conflicts are a natural part of life and can be difficult to handle. Learning how to manage emotions in conflict situations can help to improve emotional intelligence, as it allows for better understanding and management of emotions, and also helps to improve conflict resolution skills.

It's also important to learn how to manage and process difficult emotions such as grief and loss. Grief and loss can be overwhelming and can have a negative impact on emotional intelligence. It's important to learn how to process and manage these emotions in a healthy way through techniques such as therapy, journaling, talking to friends and family, and practicing self-compassion.

Emotional resilience

Another important aspect of building emotional intelligence is learning how to build and maintain emotional resilience. Emotional resilience refers to the ability to bounce back from difficult situations and to maintain emotional well-being. It can be built through practices such as mindfulness, exercise, and positive thinking. Additionally, it's important to build a support network of people you can rely on during difficult times.

Emotional intelligence is an important aspect of managing emotions.It involves being able to recognize, understand, and manage one's own emotions, as well as the emotions of others.This includes practicing mindfulness, active listening, regulating emotions, self-compassion, setting boundaries and learning how to say no, managing stress, recognizing and managing emotions in others, taking responsibility for one's own emotions, setting and achieving goals, building and maintaining healthy relationships, managing emotions in different social and cultural contexts, handling criticism and feedback, managing and expressing emotions in a professional setting, managing emotions in conflict situations, managing and processing difficult emotions, building emotional resilience and building a support network.

Remember that building emotional intelligence is a continuous process and requires continuous effort to maintain it. It's important to regularly evaluate and reflect on one's emotional intelligence, and continuously work on improving it. Additionally, seeking guidance from professionals such as therapists or coaches can also be beneficial in building emotional intelligence.

Furthermore, it's important to keep in mind that everyone is different and what works for one person may not work for another, so it's important to find what works for you. Remember that building emotional intelligence is a lifelong journey, and with the right tools and mindset, you can improve your emotional intelligence and lead a more fulfilling and healthy life. It's important to be patient with yourself and to remember that progress takes time, but with dedication and effort, you can achieve mastery over your emotions.

CHAPTER VI

Self-Compassion & Emotional Resilience

Self-compassion is the ability to be kind and understanding towards oneself during difficult times or when experiencing negative emotions. It involves treating oneself with the same understanding and care that one would offer to a good friend. Self-compassion is an important aspect of managing emotions, as it can help to reduce stress, increase well-being, and improve emotional intelligence. This chapter will focus on the importance of self-compassion and strategies for developing it.

One of the most important benefits of self-compassion is its ability to reduce stress. Stress can have a negative impact on emotional well-being and can make it more difficult to manage emotions. Self-compassion can help to reduce stress by providing a sense of understanding and acceptance towards difficult emotions, instead of judgment and criticism. This can help to create a more positive and supportive inner dialogue, which can in turn reduce stress.The benefit of self-compassion is its ability to increase well-being. Self-compassion can help to improve self-esteem and self-worth, which can in turn lead to increased well-being.

Additionally, self-compassion can also help to improve relationships, by reducing feelings of isolation and increasing feelings of connectedness.Self-compassion is also important for emotional intelligence. It allows for better understanding and management of emotions, as it promotes self-awareness and emotional regulation. Additionally, self-compassion can also help to improve communication and empathy towards others, by promoting understanding and acceptance of emotions.

Fig 1.1 (Self-Compassion & Emotional resilience)

Mindfulness

To develop self-compassion, one can practice mindfulness and self-compassion meditations. Mindfulness is the practice of being present in the moment and paying attention to one's thoughts and feelings without judgment. Self-compassion meditations often involve repeating phrases such as "May I be kind to myself" or "May I be at peace." Additionally, journaling or writing letters to oneself from a compassionate perspective can also be helpful in developing self-compassion.

Self-Compassionate Self-Talk

Another strategy for developing self-compassion is through self-compassionate self-talk. Self-compassionate self-talk involves talking to oneself in a kind and understanding way, similar to how one would talk to a good friend. This can help to change negative self-talk patterns and promote a more positive and supportive inner dialogue.It's also important to practice self-compassion in daily life by being kind and understanding towards oneself, especially during difficult times or when experiencing negative emotions. This can include taking care of oneself through self-care activities, seeking support from friends and family, and being gentle and forgiving towards oneself when making mistakes.

Emotional resilience is the ability to bounce back from difficult experiences and handle stress in a healthy way. The degree of emotional resilience depends on many factors, including age, identity, and life experiences. Building emotional resilience is an important aspect of mental health and can help individuals navigate life's challenges with greater ease.

In this chapter, we will discuss the importance of emotional resilience and strategies for building it.First and foremost, it is important to understand that emotional resilience is not the absence of negative emotions. Rather, it is the ability to cope with and process these emotions in a healthy way. Everyone experiences difficult emotions at some point in their lives, and it is important to learn how to handle these emotions in a constructive manner.

Self-Awareness

One key aspect of building emotional resilience is self-awareness. Being self-aware means having a clear understanding of your thoughts, feelings, and behaviors. This includes being aware of your triggers, patterns, and reactions to stressors. By understanding these things, you can develop strategies to manage them more effectively.Another important aspect of building emotional resilience is developing a support system. This includes having people in your life who you can talk to, confide in, and rely on for support. This can include friends, family members, or a therapist. Additionally, it is important to develop a sense of social connectedness, which can come from participating in community activities, volunteering, or joining a club or group.

Another key strategy for building emotional resilience is to practice good self-care. This includes getting enough sleep, eating well, and engaging in regular exercise. Additionally, it is important to engage in activities that promote relaxation and stress reduction, such as yoga, meditation, or deep breathing exercises.It is also important to develop a sense of perspective and to learn how to let go of things that are out of your control. This can be achieved by practicing mindfulness, which involves being present in the moment and focusing on what is happening right now, rather than dwelling on the past or worrying about the future. Additionally, it is helpful to focus on the things that you can control, rather than dwelling on things that are out of your control.

Learning How to Reframe Negative Thoughts

Another important aspect of building emotional resilience is learning how to reframe negative thoughts. This involves identifying negative thoughts, questioning their validity, and replacing them with more positive thoughts. This can be achieved through cognitive behavioral therapy (CBT) or other forms of talk therapy.

Practice Gratitude

Another way to build emotional resilience is to practice gratitude. This means taking the time to appreciate the good things in life, rather than focusing on the negative. This can be achieved by keeping a gratitude journal, where you write down things that you are grateful for each day. Additionally, sharing your gratitude with others can also be a powerful way to increase feelings of well-being.

Set Realistic Goals and Expectations

Another important aspect of building emotional resilience is learning to set realistic goals and expectations. This means setting goals that are achievable and setting realistic deadlines for achieving them. It also means being realistic about what you can accomplish in a given period of time, and avoiding over committing yourself. By setting realistic goals and expectations, you can avoid unnecessary stress and disappointment.

Building emotional resilience also involves learning how to cope with failure. Failure is an inevitable part of life and it is important to learn how to handle it in a healthy way. One way to do this is by viewing failure as a learning opportunity, rather than a personal setback. Additionally, it is important to take responsibility for your actions and to learn from your mistakes.

Promote personal growth and self-discovery.

Another way to build emotional resilience is to engage in activities that promote personal growth and self-discovery. This can include reading self-help books, engaging in therapy, or taking classes. Additionally, it is important to identify your values and to make sure that they align with the things you do in your life.

By engaging in activities that promote personal growth and self-discovery, you can develop a greater sense of self-awareness and a deeper understanding of yourself.

Manage Stress

Another key strategy for building emotional resilience is learning how to manage stress. Stress is a normal part of life, but chronic stress can have negative effects on both physical and mental health. To manage stress, it is important to engage in stress-reducing activities such as deep breathing exercises, meditation, yoga, or tai chi. Additionally, it is important to practice time management and prioritize self-care. This includes setting aside time for leisure activities, exercise, and rest.

Setting Short-Term and Long-Term Goals

It is also important to develop a sense of hope and optimism. This means maintaining a positive outlook on life and focusing on the possibilities, rather than dwelling on the negative. This can be achieved by setting short-term and long-term goals, and working towards achieving them. Additionally, it is important to surround yourself with positive people who can provide support and encouragement.

Another effective strategy for building emotional resilience is to develop a sense of purpose. This means having a sense of direction and meaning in life, and finding activities that are meaningful and fulfilling. This can be achieved by volunteering, pursuing hobbies and interests, or finding a job that aligns with your values and passions.

Practice Mindfulness

Another important strategy for building emotional resilience is to practice mindfulness, which is the ability to be present in the moment and focus on the current experience without judgment. Mindfulness can be practiced through different techniques such as meditation, yoga, tai chi, or deep breathing exercises. By practicing mindfulness, individuals can improve their ability to manage their thoughts and emotions, and increase their ability to regulate their stress response.

Ability to Adapt To Change

Building emotional resilience also involves the ability to adapt to change. Change is a constant in life and the ability to adapt to it is crucial for mental well-being. One way to adapt to change is by developing a growth mindset, which is the belief that abilities can be developed through effort and learning. This mindset encourages individuals to embrace challenges and view failures as opportunities for growth.

The strategy for building emotional resilience is learning to set boundaries. This means learning how to say "no" when necessary, setting limits on what you are willing to accept from others and making sure to prioritize your own well-being. Setting boundaries is an essential skill for protecting your mental and emotional health, and it is important to communicate these boundaries clearly and assertively.

Self-Compassion and Self-Care

Building emotional resilience also requires a certain level of self-compassion and self-care, which includes taking care of your physical, emotional, and mental well-being. This means engaging in activities that promote relaxation and stress reduction, such as yoga, meditation, or deep breathing exercises. Additionally, it is important to prioritize self-care activities like getting enough sleep, eating well, and engaging in regular exercise.

Fig 1.2 (Self-Care)

Finally, it is important to practice self-compassion. This means treating yourself with kindness and understanding, rather than being overly self-critical. This can be achieved by being mindful of negative self-talk and replacing it with more positive and supportive thoughts. Additionally, it is important to be kind and understanding towards others, and to practice empathy and compassion.

Building emotional resilience is an important aspect of mental health and well-being. It involves developing self-awareness, a support system, good self-care, a sense of perspective, reframing negative thoughts, effective communication, gratitude, setting realistic goals and expectations, coping with failure, engaging in activities that promote personal growth, practicing forgiveness, managing stress, developing a sense of hope and optimism, finding purpose, self-compassion, practicing mindfulness, adapting to change and setting boundaries. By consistently practicing these strategies, individuals can develop the ability to navigate life's challenges with greater ease, and build a stronger emotional foundation.

CHAPTER VII

Understanding and Managing Emotions in Others

Emotions are a natural part of human experience and play a vital role in our relationships and interactions with others. Understanding and managing emotions in others is an important aspect of communication and building strong relationships.

In this chapter, we will discuss the importance of understanding and managing emotions in others, and strategies for doing so.First, it is important to understand that emotions are not inherently good or bad, they are simply a natural response to different situations. However, it is important to recognize that emotions can be intense and overwhelming, and it is important to learn how to manage them in a healthy way.

Active Listening

One key aspect of understanding and managing emotions in others is active listening. This means paying close attention to what the other person is saying, both verbally and non-verbally, and responding in a way that shows you understand and care about their feelings. This includes asking open-ended questions, making reflective statements, and providing empathy.

Identify and Acknowledge Emotions

Another important aspect of understanding and managing emotions in others is learning how to identify and acknowledge emotions. This means being able to recognize different emotions and understanding the different ways they can be expressed. Additionally, it is important to acknowledge the other person's emotions, even if you do not agree with them.

Learning How to Express

Additionally, it is important to learn how to communicate effectively. This includes learning how to express your thoughts and feelings in a clear and assertive manner, as well as learning how to actively listen to others. It is also important to learn how to set boundaries, which means being able to say "no" when necessary and setting limits on what you are willing to accept from others.

Learning How to Handle Conflicts

Another important aspect of understanding and managing emotions in others is learning how to handle conflicts. Conflict is an inevitable part of human interaction, but it is important to learn how to handle it in a healthy way. One way to do this is by learning how to compromise, which means finding a solution that is acceptable to both parties. Additionally, it is important to learn how to manage anger and aggression in a constructive way.

Empathy

Another key strategy for understanding and managing emotions in others is to practice empathy. Empathy is the ability to understand and share the feelings of others. It allows individuals to see things from the perspective of others and to respond in a way that is understanding and supportive. Empathy can be practiced through different techniques such as active listening, perspective-taking, and putting oneself in the shoes of others.

Validate and Acknowledge the Emotions Of Others

Another important aspect of understanding and managing emotions in others is learning how to validate and acknowledge the emotions of others. This means recognizing that the emotions of others are valid and important, regardless of whether or not we agree with them. It also involves being able to express understanding and support for the other person's feelings.

It is also important to learn how to set emotional boundaries. This means being able to recognize when we are becoming overwhelmed or affected by the emotions of others, and taking steps to protect ourselves. This can include setting limits on the amount of time we spend with certain people, or learning how to disengage from emotionally charged conversations.

Self-Regulation

Another key strategy for understanding and managing emotions in others is to practice self-regulation. Self-regulation refers to the ability to control one's own emotions and behavior in different situations. This is important for understanding and managing emotions in others because it allows individuals to respond in a calm and composed way, rather than becoming overwhelmed or reactive.

Understand the role of cultural and societal influences

Another important strategy for understanding and managing emotions in others is to understand the role of cultural and societal influences on emotions. Different cultures and societies have different norms and expectations regarding emotions and it is important to understand and respect these differences. This means being aware of cultural and societal influences on emotions and being sensitive to the emotions of people from different cultures and backgrounds.

Provide Emotional Support

Another effective strategy for understanding and managing emotions in others is learning how to provide emotional support. This means being able to provide comfort and understanding to others during difficult times. It also means being able to provide practical support, such as helping with tasks or providing resources. Additionally, it is important to be able to provide emotional support in a non-judgmental and respectful way.

Learning How to Use Humor Effectively

Another important strategy for understanding and managing emotions in others is learning how to use humor effectively. Humor can be a powerful tool for managing emotions, as it can help diffuse tense situations, provide a sense of perspective, and create a more positive atmosphere. However, it is important to use humor in an appropriate and respectful manner, and to be aware of cultural and societal norms around humor.

Gender Norms & Trauma

It is also important to understand the role of gender and gender norms in emotions. Gender norms can influence how emotions are expressed and perceived, and it is important to be aware of these norms and to be respectful of the different ways that men and women may express their emotions.

It is also important to understand the role of trauma in emotions. Trauma can have a significant impact on the emotions of both ourselves and others, and it is important to be aware of the signs and symptoms of trauma, and to provide support and resources to those who may be struggling with the effects of trauma.

Body Language Effectively

Another important aspect of understanding and managing emotions in others is learning how to use body language effectively. Body language is a powerful tool for understanding and communicating emotions and it is important to be aware of the different cues that indicate different emotions. This includes understanding the different facial expressions, gestures, and postures that indicate different emotions, such as anger, happiness, or sadness. Additionally, it is important to be aware of one's own body language and to use it to communicate effectively.

Emotions in decision-making & communication

It is also important to understand the role of emotions in decision-making. Emotions can play a powerful role in decision-making, both positively and negatively. It is important to be aware of this and to learn how to use emotions effectively in decision-making. This includes learning how to identify and acknowledge one's own emotions, as well as understanding how emotions can influence the decision-making process. Additionally, it is important to be able to make decisions that are based on reason and logic, rather than being swayed by emotions.

It is also important to understand the role of emotions in communication, both verbal and nonverbal. Verbal communication refers to the use of words and language, and nonverbal communication refers to the use of body language, facial expressions, and other cues. Understanding how emotions are communicated verbally and nonverbally can help to improve communication and build stronger relationships.

It is also important to understand the role of emotions in problem-solving. Emotions can play a powerful role in problem-solving, both positively and negatively. It is important to be aware of this and to learn how to use emotions effectively in problem-solving. This includes learning how to identify and acknowledge one's own emotions, as well as understanding how emotions can influence the problem-solving process. Additionally, it is important to be able to solve problems that are based on reason and logic, rather than being swayed by emotions.

Emotions can play a powerful role in conflicts

It's also important to understand the role of emotions in conflict resolution. Emotions can play a powerful role in conflicts, and it is important to be aware of this and to learn how to use emotions effectively in resolving conflicts. This includes learning how to identify and acknowledge one's own emotions, as well as understanding how emotions can influence the conflict resolution process. Additionally, it is important to be able to resolve conflicts that are based on reason and logic, rather than being swayed by emotions.

It is also important to understand the role of emotions in teamwork and collaboration. Emotions can play a powerful role in teamwork and collaboration, both positively and negatively. It is important to be aware of this and to learn how to use emotions effectively in teamwork and collaboration. This includes learning how to identify and acknowledge one's own emotions, as well as understanding how emotions can influence the teamwork and collaboration process. Additionally, it is important to be able to work and collaborate effectively, rather than being swayed by emotions.

Self-Regulation

Another important strategy for understanding and managing emotions in others is learning how to regulate one's own emotions. Self-regulation is the ability to control one's own emotions, thoughts, and behaviors in different situations. This is important for understanding and managing emotions in others because it allows individuals to respond to the emotions of others in a calm and composed way, rather than becoming overwhelmed or reactive. This includes techniques such as deep breathing, mindfulness, and cognitive-behavioral therapy.

Emotions in negotiation and persuasion

It is also important to understand the role of emotions in negotiation and persuasion. Emotions can play a powerful role in negotiation and persuasion, both positively and negatively. It is important to be aware of this and to learn how to use emotions effectively in negotiation and persuasion. This includes learning how to identify and acknowledge one's own emotions, as well as understanding how emotions can influence the negotiation and persuasion process. Additionally, it is important to be able to negotiate and persuade effectively, rather than being swayed by emotions.

Emotions can play a powerful role in public speaking and presentations

It is also important to understand the role of emotions in public speaking and presentations. Emotions can play a powerful role in public speaking and presentations, both positively and negatively. It is important to be aware of this and to learn how to use emotions effectively in public speaking and presentations. This includes learning how to identify and acknowledge one's own emotions, as well as understanding how emotions can influence the public speaking and presentation process. Additionally, it is important to be able to speak and present effectively, rather than being swayed by emotions.

Finally, it is important to learn how to build and maintain relationships. This includes learning how to trust, being dependable, and being willing to forgive and be forgiven. Additionally, it is important to learn how to be open and honest in your relationships, and to build a sense of intimacy and connection.

In conclusion, understanding and managing emotions in others is an essential aspect of communication and building strong relationships. It involves active listening, identifying and acknowledging emotions, effective communication, handling conflicts, building and maintaining relationships, practicing empathy, validating and acknowledging emotions, setting emotional boundaries, practicing self-regulation, giving and receiving feedback in a constructive way, managing stress, understanding the role of cultural and societal influences, providing emotional support, understanding the role of mental health in emotions, using humor effectively, understanding the role of gender and gender norms in emotions, understanding the role of trauma in emotions, dealing with toxic emotions, using body language effectively, understanding the role of emotions in decision-making, understanding the role of emotions in communication, understanding that emotions change over time, practicing self-awareness, understanding the role of emotions in problem-solving, understanding the role of emotions in conflict resolution, understanding the role of emotions in teamwork and collaboration, regulating one's own emotions, understanding the role of emotions in negotiation and persuasion, and understanding the role of emotions in public speaking and presentations. By practicing these strategies, individuals can develop the ability to understand and manage emotions in others in a healthy and effective way, and build stronger and more fulfilling relationships.

CHAPTER VIII

The Role of Emotions in Decision Making

Emotions play a crucial role in decision making, influencing our choices and actions in both positive and negative ways. Emotions can affect our ability to process information, evaluate options, and make choices. Understanding the role of emotions in decision making is essential for making sound and rational decisions.

Affective Forecasting

One of the key ways that emotions influence decision making is through the process of affective forecasting. Affective forecasting refers to the ability to predict how we will feel in the future as a result of a particular decision. This can have a significant impact on our choices, as we are more likely to choose options that we believe will lead to positive emotions in the future. For example, if we believe that a particular job will make us happy, we are more likely to choose that job over another. However, affective forecasting can also be biased, leading us to make choices that may not be in our best interest.

Emotions can also affect our ability to process information and evaluate options. When we are in a positive emotional state, we are more likely to be open-minded, optimistic, and to weigh the pros and cons of different options. On the other hand, when we are in a negative emotional state, we are more likely to be closed-minded, pessimistic, and to focus on the negative aspects of different options. This can lead to a bias in decision making and can prevent us from considering all available options.

Costs and Benefits of Different Options

Emotions can also affect the way we weigh the costs and benefits of different options. When we are in a positive emotional state, we are more likely to be willing to take risks and to prioritize the benefits of a particular option. On the other hand, when we are in a negative emotional state, we are more likely to be risk-averse and to prioritize the costs of a particular option. This can lead to different choices and actions depending on our emotional state.

Emotions can also affect our ability to make choices by influencing our willpower and self-control. Emotions can either energize or deplete our willpower, making it more or less difficult to resist temptations and make choices that align with our goals and values. When we are in a positive emotional state, we are more likely to have the willpower to make choices that align with our goals and values. On the other hand, when we are in a negative emotional state, we are more likely to be more impulsive and to make choices that do not align with our goals and values.

Members Communicate

Furthermore, emotions can also affect the way group members communicate and give feedback to each other. When group members are in a positive emotional state, they are more likely to communicate effectively and provide constructive feedback. On the other hand, when group members are in a negative emotional state, they may be more likely to communicate poorly and provide negative feedback. This can impact the effectiveness of the group decision making process and the outcome of the decision.

Emotions Can Influence Group Decision

Additionally, emotions can also affect the way group members perceive and interpret information. When group members are in a positive emotional state, they are more likely to perceive and interpret information in a positive light. On the other hand, when group members are in a negative emotional state, they may be more likely to perceive and interpret information in a negative light. This can lead to different choices and actions depending on the emotional state of the group members.

It is important for group members to be aware of the ways that emotions can influence group decision making and to take steps to manage them. This can include techniques such as mindfulness, cognitive-behavioral therapy, and affective forecasting. Additionally, group members should be encouraged to communicate effectively, give and receive feedback in a constructive way, and to take time to reflect on their emotions before making decisions. By understanding the role of emotions in group decision making and taking steps to manage them, group members can make better decisions, and achieve their goals and aspirations.

Another important aspect of understanding the role of emotions in decision making is recognizing the impact of **cultural and societal norms**. Different cultures and societies may have different norms and expectations around emotions and how they are expressed and perceived. This can influence how emotions affect decision making, and it is important to be aware of these cultural and societal differences in order to make sound and rational decisions.

It is also important to understand the role of **mental health** in emotions and decision making. Mental health conditions such as anxiety and depression can have a significant impact on emotions, and can affect decision making. It is important to be aware of the signs and symptoms of mental health conditions, and to provide support and resources to those who may be struggling with the effects of mental health conditions.

Primary and Secondary Emotions

Another important aspect of understanding the role of emotions in decision making is learning how to distinguish between different types of emotions. There are two main types of emotions: primary and secondary emotions. Primary emotions are innate emotional responses to certain situations, such as joy, anger, sadness, and fear. Secondary emotions are emotions that are learned and developed through life experiences and socialization, such as guilt, shame, and embarrassment. It is important to be able to distinguish between primary and secondary emotions and to understand how they can affect decision making.

Primary emotions are usually more immediate and intense and can have a powerful impact on decision making, but they are also more likely to be temporary and can be regulated with emotional regulation techniques. Secondary emotions, on the other hand, tend to be more long-lasting and often stem from deeper-rooted issues and beliefs. They may require more extensive therapeutic work to be addressed.

Another important aspect of understanding the role of emotions in decision making is learning how to incorporate emotions into the decision-making process in a balanced and healthy way. This means being able to use emotions as a source of information, but not allowing them to completely dictate decisions. It is important to use critical thinking and rational analysis to evaluate the pros and cons of different options, while also considering the emotional implications of each decision. This can be achieved by taking a step back and analyzing the situation objectively, and by considering the long-term consequences of a decision, rather than just the immediate emotional response.

In addition, it is important to seek feedback and support from others when making important decisions. Seeking feedback from others can provide valuable perspectives and insight into the decision-making process. Additionally, support from others can help individuals to manage emotions and make sound decisions. This can include seeking the advice of a therapist, counselor, or coach.

Impulsive Decisions

Another important strategy in understanding the role of emotions in decision making is learning how to delay impulsive decisions. Impulsive decisions are often made based on emotions rather than rational thinking. By learning how to delay impulsive decisions, individuals can take the time to evaluate the situation objectively and make decisions that align with their goals and values. This can be achieved by using techniques such as the "5 second rule" which involves counting backwards from five before making a decision, or the "ten-minute rule" which involves waiting ten minutes before making a decision. By taking the time to delay impulsive decisions, individuals can make better decisions that align with their goals and values.

In conclusion, understanding the role of emotions in decision making is an essential aspect of making sound and rational decisions. It involves recognizing the impact of affective forecasting, understanding how emotions can affect our ability to process information, evaluate options, and make choices, being aware of the role of emotions in group decision making, recognizing the impact of cultural and societal norms, understanding the role of mental health in emotions and decision making, developing a strong emotional intelligence, distinguishing between primary and secondary emotions, incorporating emotions into the decision-making process in a balanced and healthy way, practicing mindfulness and self-awareness, seeking feedback and support from others, delaying impulsive decisions, and managing stress. By being aware of these factors and taking steps to manage emotions in decision making, individuals can make better decisions, navigate the complexities of emotions, and achieve their goals and aspirations. It's important to remember that understanding and managing emotions in decision making is an ongoing process that requires practice and effort, and seeking support when needed. By developing strategies such as delaying impulsive decisions, practicing stress management techniques, and incorporating emotions into the decision-making process in a balanced and healthy way, individuals can make decisions that not only align with their rational thoughts and goals, but also take into account their emotional well-being and overall satisfaction. Additionally, by seeking feedback and support from others, learning how to manage stress, and recognizing the impact of cultural and societal norms, individuals can make better decisions that take into account the perspectives and experiences of others.

CHAPTER IX

Difference between IQ and EQ

Emotional quotient (EQ), or Emotional intelligence, is defined as an individual's ability to identify, evaluate, control, and express their emotions. People with high EQ often make great leaders and team players because of their ability to understand, empathize, and connect with those around them.

Intelligence quotient (IQ), is a score obtained from one of several standardized tests designed to assess a person's intelligence.

IQ is used to determine academic achievement and identify individuals with exceptional intelligence or intellectual disabilities. Emotional quotient (EQ), or Emotional intelligence is a better indicator of workplace success and is used to identify leaders, great teams his players, and people who work best alone.

Difference between IQ and EQ

Many people think that IQ is more important for a person to be successful in life, but researchers believe that people with higher EQs are more successful in their careers. Therefore, it is one of the great research topics for societal reforms and for human intelligent behavior.

Meaning

Intelligence Quotient, or IQ, is a number obtained from standardized intelligence tests that describes a person's ability to think logically.EQ refers to a person's level of emotional intelligence as represented by scores obtained on standardized tests.

Measures

- **IQ**-General Intelligence
- **EQ**-Emotional Intelligence

Acquisition

- **IQ**-It is an inborn ability.
- **EQ**-It is learned and improved ability.

Ability

- **IQ**-Learn, understand and practice knowledge, logical thinking and abstract thinking.
- **EQ**-Recognizing, controlling and expressing one's own emotions and recognizing and appreciating the emotions of others.

Ensures

- **IQ**-Success in school.
- **EQ**-Success in life.

Recognizes

- **IQ**-People with high intelligence, common sense, mental problems, etc.
- **EQ**-Executives, captains, managers, people with social challenges..

Origin

- **IQ**-1883, English statistician Francis Galton's paper "Inquiries into Human Faculty and Its Development" First application came in French psychologist Alfred Binet's 1905 test to assess school children in France.
- **EQ**-1985, Wayne Payne's doctoral thesis "A Study of Emotion: Developing Emotional Intelligence" Popular use came in Daniel Goleman's 1995 book "Emotional Intelligence - Why it can matter more than IQ"

Popular Tests

- **IQ**-Stanford-Binet test; Wechsler; Woodcock-Johnson Tests of Cognitive Abilities.
- **EQ**-Mayer-Salovey-Caruso Test (emotion-based problem-solving tasks); Daniel Goleman model Score (based on emotional competencies).

EMOTIONAL INTELLIGENCE IN THE WORKPLACE

Emotional intelligence is important at work as it enables us to perceive, reason, understand and manage our own and others' emotions. When you learn to control your emotions, you will be able to lead and help others, and you will be happier and more successful.In many case at work, emotional intelligence plays an important role. It has been shown that people with a high emotional quotient at work are happier at work because they are better at managing themselves and their relationships, and because they are more productive.

Many tasks in an organization are solved through collaboration with others, and clear communication is an important aspect of teamwork. Understanding others and managing their emotions while interacting with them helps build better connections that enable them to function smoothly in situations that arise in the workplace.From a leader's perspective, this becomes an important set of skills that enable the development of a more harmonious work environment. By strengthening the connections between teams and allowing them to build engagement through these skills, they improve the work culture within the organization and increase productivity.

Here's is some listed why emotional intelligence is important in the workplace.

- **Understanding Nonverbal Communication:** You have the opportunity to correct the situation before it becomes a problem. For example, if you notice that a colleague is showing nonverbal signs of sadness, you can put that colleague aside and show empathy.

- **Be aware of personal feelings:** Use this skill to adjust your behavior before it becomes a problem for clients or colleagues. For example, if you know you had a tough night, you can try changing your behavior the next day by shifting your focus to more positive emotions.
- **Increased efficiency:** Being empathetic and understanding the emotions of others can help you make decisions more easily and complete tasks more efficiently.
- **Career advancement:** Emotional intelligence and leadership skills go hand in hand. By actively demonstrating skills such as patience, active listening, positivity, and empathy, you can be promoted to leadership roles, earn promotions and pay raises.
- **Encourage others to develop strong interpersonal skills:** Emotions are contagious, and demonstrating explicit motivation, empathy, responsibility, and teamwork can encourage team participation.

Benefits of Emotional intelligence in the workplace

- Working towards the organization's goals regardless of obstacles that arise.
- Greater motivation among staff to understand their own emotions and those of their colleagues.
- Healthy communication that produces common goals across the business.
- The workforce having a positive outlook when it comes to the job at hand.
- Positive relationships and deeper connections between employees.
- Flexibility; high EI means employees can respond to change effectively and handle any additional stress it brings.
- Improved efficiencies with empathetic staff making decisions based on what is best for everyone involved.
- Career progression, staff with high EI are likely to excel in leadership positions.

IMPROVING EI IN THE WORKPLACE

There are many ways to improve Emotional intelligence and make it a more important part of an organization works.

1. **Understand your emotions**

- First, focus on the first pillar and learn how to recognize and understand your emotions.
- How are you currently feeling about your work and relationships with colleagues?
- How do these feelings affect the people around you?
- Do you allow negative emotions to affect how you interact with colleagues and how you work?

Being more aware of these factors is essential to improving your emotional intelligence. An easy tool to start with is to name the emotions you feel when they occur. This will help you recognize them in the future and track where they influence your behavior.Once you start naming and tracking your emotions, you will be able to assess your weaknesses. It's when negative emotions (anger, frustration, concern, fear, overwhelm, jealousy, inadequacy, etc.) cloud your judgment and you can't admit your best.

1. **Get feedback**

It can be difficult to understand your emotions on your own. When it comes to self-analysis, we often have blind spots and struggle to see for ourselves what seems easy to others.

Seek a second opinion to overcome this and ensure your results are not biased. This could be a boss, co-worker, friend, family member, or anyone else who knows you well and can provide helpful information on how to respond to different situations depending on your mood and emotional state. You may discover some hard truths that you don't like or want to hear. But learning to accept criticism without being offended or defensive is another important part of developing emotional intelligence, and it leads to two lessons in one.

3. **Respond don't react**

Many people are prone to outbursts and outbursts of anger when disagreements and conflicts arise in the workplace. Emotionally intelligent people learn to keep their cool even in stressful situations. Instead of reacting impulsively, taking some time to understand your feelings and reacting more calmly will move you closer to solving the situation rather than making it worse.

4. **Active listening**

Listening to and paying attention to nonverbal cues is important for developing emotional intelligence. Waiting your turn without taking the time to listen to your colleagues is a quick way to cause problems at work. Active listening helps you avoid misunderstandings, shows respect for the speaker, and maximizes your chances of responding appropriately. It's also a great starting point for employees to improve their communication skills.

5. **Practice**

Unfortunately, emotional intelligence is not easy. Nor is it a single one. Instead, it is a set of skills that require constant practice. Therefore, continuous training is required to truly develop EI and develop emotional management skills. EI requires a high degree of self-analysis, which often means acting differently than your first instincts.

IMPLEMENTING EI IN THE WORKPLACE

- Start with yourself
- Identify employee strengths and weaknesses
- Define workplace policies

- Give employees a voice
- Assertion training
- Deal with stress
- Employee development
- Encourage employees to share their emotions
- Regular and factual feedback

Emotional Intelligence Matters in Leadership

Emotional intelligence is important for several reasons. Emotional intelligent leaders are able to develop and maintain a positive, productive and efficient workplace while constantly motivating employees to do their best.

Leaders with this critical skill can create a work environment where employees feel comfortable taking risks and sharing ideas. You can make difficult decisions, resolve conflicts effectively, and adapt to changing business objectives and situations.

A lack of emotional intelligence hinders a leader's ability to collaborate and communicate effectively with others. When leaders cannot control their emotions, employees are less likely to share their ideas and are less likely to reach their full potential.

CHAPTER X

Emotional Trauma

From the moment that you were born, you've been learning about your emotions. You may have learned about your emotions as a baby, but it's important to learn how to identify and understand them now so that you can use them in healthy ways.

The most common symptoms of emotional trauma are:

- Constant fearfulness
- Flashbacks
- Anxiety
- Depression

TRAUMATIC

The traumatic event is not necessarily a personal physical experience. Any experience that arouses intense negative emotions, such as seeing, observing, or hearing something, can be traumatic. Determining whether something is traumatic is not based on each individual's subjective emotional reaction to the event. The depth of trauma is related to the intensity of negative emotions felt about the experience. In other words, the same experience can affect different people differently. It may be traumatic for you, but not for others. Causes of Emotional and Psychological Trauma:

Symptoms of Trauma

When observing and considering reactions to trauma, it is important to remember that these are normal reactions to unusual events. There is no "right" or "wrong" way to feel or react to these situations. We all think differently and have different perspectives, conditioning, and physical and emotional reactions. Emotional and psychological symptoms:

- Shock, Denial, Or Disbelief
- Confusion, Difficulty Concentrating
- Anger, Frustration, Mood Swings
- Anxiety And Fear
- Guilt, Shame, Self-Blame
- Withdrawal From Others
- Feeling Sad Or Hopeless
- Feeling Disconnected Or Numb
- Physical Symptoms:
- Insomnia Or Nightmares
- Malaise
- Easily Startled, Difficulty Concentrating, Fast Heartbeat

Tension And Excitement, Discomfort And Pain

How to Heal Emotional Trauma

Healing from psychological and emotional trauma is an individual experience. What works for one person may not work for another. Below are options to help you move toward healing, but the path is certainly not the same for everyone. Advice will help you find your way.Most people experience emotional trauma at some point in their life. Emotional trauma is a common condition that can affect anyone. Sufferers experience triggered feelings when thinking about their traumatic event- this is referred to as **post-trauma syndrome**.

Triggered emotions can cause serious health issues for trauma victims. These include depression, substance abuse, and anxiety disorders. It's important to recognize when someone is suffering from post-trauma syndrome so they can receive the help they need. It's also important to console and support sufferers when they're ready to talk about their experiences.Trauma sufferers may feel multiple emotions after experiencing a traumatic event. They may feel anger, guilt, sadness, or other strong feelings towards their perpetrator. Remaining detached from these feelings is crucial for recovery.

The **emotional trauma of abuse** can be extremely difficult to overcome. And it is only through the help of a therapist that one can begin to move forward with life. Recovery from emotional trauma will not be easy, but with the right resources, it can be done. The good news is that emotional trauma does not have to last forever. There are many things you can do to help yourself heal from it.

Overcome From Emotional Trauma

1. **Identify your feelings:** It's important to identify how you're feeling in order to understand what happened, why it happened and what action(s) need to be taken in order for things to improve.

2. **Talk about your feelings:** Talking helps release tension, relieve stress and reduce anxiety. It also allows people who are close to you (like friends) to listen without judging or criticizing, which is important because they will be there with support as well as an ear when needed.

3. **Get professional help:** If talking doesn't seem like enough or if there's still some unresolved issues then professional help may be necessary, especially if there are long-lasting effects such as depression or anxiety disorders that need treatment and therapy sessions may also be helpful depending on the case

4. Use your best judgment to make decisions in spite of past experiences in similar situations.

5. Ask for help from others who can give you support and encouragement for your healing process; ask for their help in finding solutions to problems related to your feelings about what happened to you.

6. Start a journal about all the things that made you feel good about yourself, and all the bad things that made you feel bad about yourself, so you can see how much self-esteem is really dependent on each situation.

7. Listen to music in particular because it can help with memory and focus, and also because it's fun!

8. Stop comparing yourself to other people, even if their life looks better than yours does at first glance. You're not going to become them, no matter how much you want to be like them!

9. Make sure your friends are supportive of your recovery process by not excluding them from your life when they ask why you seem so depressed or angry or distant while they themselves feel happy and carefree all the time because they're never sad or angry or distant anymore!

10. Admit fault and take responsibility for it when necessary (but only if that was an appropriate response). Don't use excuses like "But I didn't know..." or "I was only doing what everyone else did." People

11. Forgive yourself for what happened and move forward with your life without dwelling on the past too much. You can't change what happened in the past, but you can start making better decisions for yourself in the future so that hopefully this won't happen again!

In conclusion, the book "Emotional Intelligence: What it Takes to be and Why it is Important" provides a comprehensive overview of emotional intelligence and its significance in both personal and professional life. The author delves into the key components of emotional intelligence and provides practical tips on how to develop and improve these skills. The conclusion highlights the importance of emotional intelligence in enhancing one's relationships, career, and overall well-being. It emphasizes that emotional intelligence can be developed and improved with effort and practice and encourages readers to take an active role in building their emotional intelligence. The book serves as a valuable resource for anyone seeking to better understand and enhance their emotional intelligence.

References And Bibliography

• Dr Axe Limbic System Available from: https://draxe.com/health/limbic-system/ (accessed 28.12.2020)

• Live science Teen brain facts Available from:https://www.livescience.com/21461-teen-brain-adolescence-facts.html (accessed 28.10.2020)

• Adolphs, Ralph, and David J Anderson. The Neuroscience Of Emotion. Reprint, Princeton, NJ: Princeton University Press., 2018.

• Tottenham, Nim. \"The Brain'S Emotional Development | Dana Foundation\". Dana Foundation, 2017. https://www.dana.org/article/the-brains-emotional-development/.

• Walsh, Jeffrey. Youtube.Com, 2013. https://www.youtube.com/watch?v=GDlDirzOSI8.

• Clark, Robert. \"The Thalamus – Feelings And Emotions\". Sites.Google.Com, 2014. https://sites.google.com/site/racinstr001/the-thalamus.

• Beadle, J. N., D. Tranel, N. J. Cohen, and M. C. Duff. \"Empathy In Hippocampal Amnesia\". Frontiers In Psychology 4 (2013). doi:10.3389/fpsyg.2013.00069.

• Kropotov, Juri D. \"Affective System, Emotions, And Stress\". Functional Neuromarkers For Psychiatry, 2016, 207-229. doi:10.1016/b978-0-12-410513-3.00013-9.

• Lane, R.D., and L. Nadel. \"APA Psycnet\". Psycnet.Apa.Org, 2000. https://psycnet.apa.org/record/2000-08961-000.

• Bar-On, R. (1997). The Emotional Quotient Inventory (EQ-i): Technical manual. Toronto, Canada: Multi-Health Systems,

• Inc.

• Bar-On, R. (2006). The Bar-On model of emotional-social intelligence (ESI). Psicothema, 18 (1), 13-25.

• Callahan, J. & McCollum, E. (2002). Conceptualizations of emotion research in organizational contexts. Advances in

• Developing Human Resources, 4(1), 4-21.

• Fernández-Berrocal, P. & Extremera, N. (2006). Emotional intelligence: A theoretical and empirical review of its first 15

• years of history. Psycotherma, 18, 7-12.

• Goleman, D. (n.d.). Daniel Goleman. Retrieved from http://www.danielgoleman.info/topics/emotional-intelligence/

• Goleman, D. (1998). Working with emotional intelligence. Santa Ana, CA: Books on Tape.

• Goleman, D., Boyatzis, R. & McKee, A. (2010). L'Intelligence émotionnelle au travail. Paris, France: Pearson- Village

• Mondial.

• Jensen, E. (2005). Teaching with the brain in mind. Alexandria, VA: Association of Supervision and Curriculum

• Development.

• Paul, A. M. (1999, June 28). Promotional intelligence. Salon. Retrieved from

• https://www.salon.com/1999/06/28/emotional/

• Payne, W. (1986). A study of emotion: Developing emotional intelligence; self-integration, relating to fear, pain and

• desire. Ann Arbor, MI: UMI.

• Salovey, P. & Mayer, J. (1990). Emotional intelligence. Imagination, Cognition and Personality, 1, 9, 185-211.

• Schulze, R. & Roberts, R. (Eds.) (2005). Emotional intelligence: An international handbook. Cambridge, MA: Hogrefe &

• Huber.

• Sewell, G. F. (2011, March-April). How emotional intelligence can make a difference. Military Review. Retrieved from

• http://www.armyupress.army.mil/Portals/7/military-review/Archives/English/MilitaryReview_20110430_art012.pdf

• Spielberger, Ch. (2004). The encyclopedia of applied psychology. Oxford, MS: Elsevier Academic Press.

• Taylor-Clark, T. M. (2015). Emotional intelligence competencies and the army leadership requirements model (Master's

• Thesis, U.S. Army Command and General Staff College, Fort Leavenworth, KS).

• https://core.ac.uk/download/pdf/235850833.pdf

• https://www.teachthought.com/pedagogy/tone-teaching/

Figure references:

• https://d26toa8f6ahusa.cloudfront.net/wp-content/uploads/2021/05/13134725/Picture1-6-768x299.png

• https://www.self.com/story/emotional-regulation-skills

• https://upload.wikimedia.org/wikiversity/en/a/a1/Blog_prefrontal_cortex.jpg

• Sportslab.Net.Nz, 2019. https://sportslab.net.nz/wp-content/uploads/2019/07/limbic-system.jpg.

• https://visitmhp.com/wp-content/uploads/2022/03/thoughts-and-its-relationship-with-emotions-300x292.png.webp

• https://www.mbaknol.com/wp-content/uploads/2014/01/emotional-intelligence-four-branch-model-mbaknol.jpg.webp

• https://www.wellbeingcenter.co/admin2/uploads/blue-and-gray-maximalist-technology-instagram-post-(69).jpg

Printed by Libri Plureos GmbH in Hamburg,
Germany